13th
BOY

13th
BOY

Tony
11
SangEun Lee

13th BOY♥ CONTENTS

13TH BOY

DDARRRRNG (DRIIIING)
HEE-SO EUN!
WAKE UP!
IT'S LUNCH TIME!!
LET'S GO EAT! HURRY UP!
DO YOU KNOW TODAY'S MENU? IS THERE MEAT?
BOOSHISHI (DAZE)
...I THINK IT'S PORK CUTLET...
AHHH—! FOR SOME REASON I'M SO HUNGRY TODAY! I EVEN FEEL DIZZY!
HFF!
HFF!
KORRRK (RUMBLE)

......
LET'S GO ALREADY—! OTHERWISE, I MIGHT EAT YOU.
HE DIDN'T COME TO SCHOOL.
HEH! I KNOW, I KNOW... I LOOK DELICIOUS.
WHAT'S UP? WHAT'RE YOU LOOKING AT?
WHIE-YOUNG JANG? BEING LATE IS NORMAL FOR HIM...
UM, NOTHING.
... AND ...
JUST LOOKS LIKE WHIE-YOUNG'S SKIPPED SCHOOL TODAY.
...HUH? ♪
WHY'RE YOU SUDDENLY INTERESTED IN HIM?

I-INTERESTED?! NO, NO...
IT'S JUST THAT I HAPPENED TO RUN INTO HIM COMING TO SCHOOL THIS MORNING... TOOOTALLY BY CHANCE!
WE WALKED TOGETHER FOR MOST OF THE WAY, BUT I LEFT HIM BEHIND 'COS I THOUGHT I WAS GONNA BE LATE.
SO SINCE HE NEVER GOT HERE, I WAS JUST WONDERING... AS A CLASS-MATE.
HMMMMMM~?
WHAT'S WITH THAT LOOK OF BLATANT DISTRUST? WHAT'D I DO?!!
WHEN HEE-SO'S INTERESTED IN A DUDE, IT'S ALWAYS ONE OF THE FOLLOWING—
①SHE'S GOT HER EYE ON HIM. ②SHE'S GOT A CRUSH ON HIM. ③SHE'S GOT FEELINGS FOR HIM.
THEY'RE ALL THE SAME! GIMME A WIDER RANGE OF OPTIONS!
I WAS THINKING IT'S BEEN A WHILE SINCE YOU GOT DUMPED BY WON-JUN~!
WELL, IT'S ABOUT TIME YOU WENT ON THE HUNT FOR A NEW MAN.
SO IT'S WHIE-YOUNG NOW?
WH-WHAT THE HELL ARE YOU TALKING ABOUT?! WOULD YOU SHUT UP?!
WELL, ANYWAY...

...JUN-BAE SAW HIM ON THE WAY HERE.
*<JUN-BAE SEO> A CLASSMATE WHO LIKES NAM-JOO
HE WAS LOOKING OUT THE WINDOW OF THE BUS, AND HE SAW WHIE-YOUNG HEADING AWAY FROM SCHOOL.
THAT GUY'S A WEIRDO.
I DON'T UNDERSTAND WHY HE'S EVEN ENROLLED IN SCHOOL.
YEAH...
HE'S GOT A LOT OF ISSUES.
HE ALWAYS GETS HERE AFTER FIRST OR SECOND PERIOD, AND A LOT OF THE TIME HE SKIPS ENTIRELY.
AND WHEN HE *IS* HERE? HE SLEEPS ALL DAY.
I HEARD HE EVEN SLEEPS THROUGH EXAMS.
IT'S NOT A GOOD IDEA TO GET CLOSE TO HIM.

LAND MINE...?
HE'S LIKE A LAND MINE—YOU NEVER KNOW WHEN HE'S GONNA GO OFF...
HE'S OUTTA CONTROL.
HMM...
DON'T YOU THINK YOU'RE BEING TOO HARD ON HIM?
I DON'T THINK HE'S ALL THAT BAD.
WHA?!
ACTUALLY, HE'S HELPED ME OUT A BUNCH OF TIMES. HE'S GOT THOSE MEAN EYES, BUT...
...HE'S NOT THAT TERRIBLE IF YOU REALLY GET TO KNOW HIM. HE'S NOT GOOD AT SAYING NO...
......
I KNEW IT...
YOU'RE TOTALLY INTO WHIE-YOUNG JANG!
NO!! NEVER!!

WHEN HE'S IN SCHOOL, ALL HE DOES...
...IS ACT COLD—AND IGNORE EVERYONE ELSE.
EXCUSE ME, I'M COLLECTING HOMEWORK...
YOU'D BETTER NOT BE. I CAN'T APPROVE OF HIM!
WHEN DID YOU GET SO CLOSE TO HIM? AND HE HELPED YOU, FOR REAL? THAT'S A SHOCKER.
ARE WE LIVING ON THE SAME PLANET?
...NO WAY...
HE'S NOT THAT HARD TO TALK TO.
HE GIVES OFF THIS AURA, LIKE HE DOESN'T WANNA GET INVOLVED WITH ANYONE.
SO EVERYONE'S RELUCTANT TO APPROACH HIM.

BUT YOU'RE SAYING HE GOES EASY ON YOU?
EHH...?

HUUH~? SINCE WHEN DID YOU TWO BECOME BESTIES? HE'S NOT EVEN FRIENDS WITH ANY GUYS—
AND HE NEVER GIVES THE TIME OF DAY TO THE GIRLS. HE MUST THINK PRETTY HIGHLY OF YOU, HUH?
CAN'T YOU SEE?
I'VE NEVER IGNORED YOU, NOT EVEN ONCE.
H-HE DOESN'T! HE'S DEFINITELY PRICKLY.
WHENEVER I TALK TO HIM, HE USUALLY JUMPS ON ME OR YELLS AT ME.
HE DOESN'T LIKE ANYTHING I DO. AND HE ALWAYS TEASES ME AND NEVER COMPLIMENTS ME...

IT'S NATURAL TO NOT BE ABLE TO GET SOMETHING LIKE THAT OUT OF MY HEAD!
I THOUGHT IT DIDN'T MATTER HOW HE SAW ME, BUT...
IT'D BE BETTER...
...TO BE MADLY IN LOVE WITH YOU.
...ANYWAY, YOU CAN THINK ABOUT IT LATER...
...SO LET'S GO EAT NOW, PLEASE?
KOORRRRK (RUMBLE)
......
...DOES IT MATTER...?
I WANT TO KNOW! I WANT TO KNOW WHAT'S GOING ON IN HIS HEAD!
TAK (TMP)

SORRY, NAM-JOO! I GOTTA GO SOMEWHERE, SO FEEL FREE TO EAT MY LUNCH TOO.
I GOTTA KNOW RIGHT NOW!!
WHERE THE HELL ARE YOU GOING? THE CAFETERIA IS THIS WAY!!
SHOULDA KNOWN SHE'D PICK THE DUDE OVER A FRIEND, HUH? DANGIT...
KORRRRK (RUMBLE)
IF I'M RIGHT...
두리번
DOORIBUN
HFF...
HFF...
두리번
DOORIBUN (LOOK)

OTHER THAN HIS HOUSE AND SCHOOL, THE ONLY OTHER PLACE I CAN THINK OF...
...IS HERE...
...HE SHOULD BE HERE...
THERE!
...IS THAT HIM? IT'S TOO FAR TO TELL, BUT IT MUST BE, HUH?

KOORRRR (RUMBLE)
...AW...
RAIN...?
TOOK (PLIP)
톡
TOOK
톡
톡
TOOK
TOOK
톡
LISTEN, MASTER.
DO YOU KNOW WHAT I DREAM EVERY NIGHT?

I ALWAYS HEAR A VOICE.
NIGHT AFTER NIGHT, IT SAYS THE SAME THING.
BE HER FRIEND IN MY PLACE.
STAY BESIDE HER SO SHE ISN'T LONELY.
TAKE CARE OF HER.
IT'S...
...YOUR VOICE, ISN'T IT, MASTER?
YOU REALLY DO LIKE HEE...
WHIE-YOUNG JANG!!
WHACK (SWISH)

HEE-SO EUN...? WHY...
WHAT'RE YOU DOING HERE?
IT'S STARTING TO RAIN. IF YOU DON'T MOVE, YOU'LL...
...GET WET...
SWAHHHH (FWSSSSH)
......

쏴아
SWAHHHH
WOW—! IT'S COMING DOWN IN BUCKETS! I'M SOAKED.
ACHOO!
......
쏴아
SWAHHHH
L-LET'S GET UNDER THE BRIDGE FOR NOW!

THE SAME GOES FOR YOU TOO!
YOU SKIPPED SCHOOL, AND YOU'RE TAKING AN UNPRODUCTIVE NAP HERE!
WHY ARE YOU HERE? AREN'T YOU S'POSED TO BE IN SCHOOL?
ARE YOU HERE TO SCOLD ME?
THEN YOU'RE BEING JUST AS UNPRODUCTIVE AS I AM.
BESIDES, I WASN'T SLEEPING.
THE REASON I CAME HERE IS 'COS I CAN'T STAND IT ANYMORE!
GIMME A STRAIGHT ANSWER!
ANYWAY, WE'RE STUCK HERE TILL THE RAIN STOPS.

I WANT TO HEAR THE TRUTH!
WHAT DID YOU MEAN WHEN YOU SAID IT'D BE BETTER IF YOU WERE IN LOVE WITH ME?
HOW DO YOU REALLY FEEL ABOUT ME?
IF YOU KNEW...
...WHAT WOULD YOU DO?
IF I TELL YOU I LIKE YOU...
...WHAT'RE YOU GONNA DO ABOUT IT?

DID YOU ALREADY MAKE UP YOUR MIND ABOUT THAT BEFORE ASKING ME?
...MY MIND?
MY MIND... ...UMM, WELL...
IF YOU CONFESS TO ME... THEN WHAT...?
DAMN, HE'S NOT MAKING THIS EASY!!
SERIOUSLY, WHAT SHOULD I DO...?
WHAT DIFFERENCE DOES IT MAKE IF YOU KNOW HOW I FEEL WHEN YOU HAVEN'T GOT A PLAN?
PFFT!
...SHALL WE TEST THEM?
OUR FEELINGS FOR EACH OTHER.
NOW I GET IT.
THE HEART I GOT FROM YOU, MASTER...
...IT'S...
......
...I WANT TO KNOW TOO.

...AND TOUCH HER...
IF I LIKED SOMEONE, I'D...
...WANT TO REACH OUT...
...RIGHT?
WHAT...?!
I'M GOING TO KISS YOU, SO IF YOU DON'T WANT TO...
...DUCK, PUSH ME BACK, OR RUN.
BUT WHACKING ME'S OUT.

WHERE SHOULD I RUN TO?!!
WHAT IS HE DOING...?
......
HANG ON! AGAIN?!
H...

IF YOU HATE IT, PUSH ME AWAY.
I MEAN...
...I...

쏴아ㆍ

SHWAAAH
(FWSHHHH)

...DON'T HATE IT.

MUNG (DAZE)
멍~...
WHAT...
WHAT DID I DO?!!

I KISSED WHIE-YOUNG JANG!!
AARRGHHH...
THAT'S RIGHT. IT WAS RAINING, AND EVERYTHING WENT HAYWIRE.
I'D LIKE TO THINK I MADE A MISTAKE 'COS OF THE MOOD, BUT...
AAAHHHHH...
...SHALL WE TEST THEM?
OUR FEELINGS FOR EACH OTHER.
...THAT DIRTY, ROTTEN SCOUNDREL TRICKED ME...
IT WAS MORE THAN THAT...
...IT WASN'T JUST ONCE...

IT HAPPENED SEVERAL TIMES ...!!
AT THE END, HE SAID...
AND I WAS CLINGING TO HIM INSTEAD OF RESISTING...

"HEH" ...?
REALLY, "HEH" ...?
I WAS EXPECTING AT LEAST ONE PUNCH, BUT IT LOOKS LIKE YOU ENJOYED YOURSELF.
HEH!
HE WENT "HEH"... AT ME...
NOOOOOOO...
...AND I FELT A HORRIFIC SENSE OF DEFEAT, LIKE I'D JUST BEEN PLAYED!!
I'M SO ANGRY, ASHAMED, AND FURIOUS!!
UARRRGH!

WHAT HAPPENED TO YOUR FACE, HEE-SO?
YOUR EYES ARE ALL SUNKEN!
BUT THE WORST PART OF IT IS...
...IT'S 'COS OF A DREAM I HAD LAST NIGHT.
MORE LIKE A NIGHTMARE.
QWENG (HOLLOW)
A NIGHT-MARE? WAS IT FULL OF GHOSTS?
N-NO, IT WAS...
MY DREAM WAS ALL ABOUT HAVING SEX WITH WHIE-YOUNG!!
UUURGH...

NO, NO! THIS CAN'T BE HAP-PENING!!
KWANG KWANG (BANG) KWANG KWANG
H-HOW SCARY WAS IT?!
I BLAME IT ALL ON THE BOOKS IN MY ROOM.
SECRET DESIRE
FIRE IN THE DESERT
BURNING TOGETHER
BODY PARADISE
MY FLESH CRIES OUT
THE NIGHT THAT BURNS IN OUR FLESH
NAKED ROMANCE
A NIGHT OF PASSION
THE FIRST TIME
SWEET PLEASURE
THERE WAS NAKED FLESH EVERYWHERE (?), AND IT WAS BEYOND EMBARRASSING...
A SECRET IN THE NIGHT
TWO BECOMING ONE
DARK DESIRES
SILVERY WAVES OF MALIBU
HEAVY BREATHING
BODY GAME
WHOA, WHIE-YOUNG JANG!
TCH!
IS THIS A ONE-WOMAN SHOW?
SOMETIMES YOU DO THE MOST BIZARRE THINGS.
SHUWOO (HISSS)
WHAT'RE YOU DOING?

WHIE-YOUNG JANG...
?
THAT VIVID DREAM OF SKIN-ON-SKIN FROM LAST NIGHT!!
화악!
WHAAK (BLUSH)
...WHAT'S WRONG WITH HER?
H-HOW WOULD I KNOW?
AARRRRGH...
WHAT'S THAT ALL ABOUT?
HE CAME TO SCHOOL ON TIME.
NO, NO, NO!!
IT'S THE SECOND TIME I'VE TALKED TO HIM.
IT CAN'T BE!!
OKAY, NOW TURN TO PAGE 178.
LET'S START BY READING TH PASSAGE.

<I'M A BOY. YOU'RE A GIRL. WE ARE STUDENTS.>
<WE ARE THE FUTURE. WHEN BOY MEETS GIRL...>
<...WE SEE THE POWER OF LOVE. I LOVE YOU SO MUCH.>
DAMMIT... I CAN'T FOCUS.
IT'S ALL BECAUSE OF HIM!
I SHOULDN'T HAVE LET HIM PLAY ME YESTERDAY...
IF I HADN'T KISSED HIM...
...I WOULDN'T BE SO FREAKED OUT RIGHT NOW!!
HE... DOESN'T SEEM TO CARE ABOUT YESTERDAY AT ALL.
PLAYING A GAME IN THE MIDDLE OF CLASS
IT'S LIKE THROWING A ROCK INTO A QUIET STREAM!!
HOW COME HE'S SO CALM?!!
HE KISSED ME!!

YAAAY~! ♫~ HE'S REALLY NOT COMING—?!! DO WE HAVE TO PLAY DODGE-BALL, THOUGH? ♪
I HATE DODGE-BALL!
LET'S JUST PLAY!!
<ANNOUNCEMENT FROM THE CLASS REP> THE TEACHER CAN'T BE HERE TODAY, SO THE BOYS SHOULD PLAY SOCCER, AND THE GIRLS DODGEBALL.
WE SHOULD DIVIDE INTO TEAMS, SO WOULD YOU ALL GATHER HERE?
WHY AM I THE ONLY ONE WHO'S ALL MIXED-UP?!!
WHAT'S UP? HE NEVER COMES TO GYM CLASS.
AH! IT'S WHIE-YOUNG! HE'S HERE!!
WOW!!
OYOK!!
EH?
HUH?
I DON'T WANNA...
SHALL WE FINISH OUR COMPETITION?
HMM~! DODGE-BALL AGAIN.

EHHH—?! IT'S TRUE. WHY'S HE HERE? HE USUALLY SLEEPS IN THE NURSE'S OFFICE DURING GYM.
I WANNA WATCH!!
SO IS HE GONNA PLAY SOCCER?
KYAAAH—!
CHUK (TAK)
척
KWANG (ROAR)
콰왕
OKAY! LET'S DO THIS, HEE-SO!!
YOUR SPARK SHOT AND MY AXE SHOT!!!
AHHH... I'M TIRED...;;
SHOULD I TAKE CARE OF THIS IDIOT ...?
JIKUN (THROB)
지끈
WHAT'S WRONG WITH ME? I CAN'T IGNORE HIM, AND I CAN'T KEEP MY EYES OFF HIM... IT'S GIVING ME A HEADACHE!!

WHAT? YOU'RE NOT GONNA PLAY?
EXCUSE US, YOU GUYS, WE'RE GONNA STAY OUT OF IT, SO...
...YOU TWO CAN PLAY HOWEVER YOU WANT.
WHA?
YEAH, THAT'S RIGHT! WE'LL ONLY GET IN YOUR WAY OTHER-WISE.
HAVE FUN, YOU TWO.
THEN WHY DON'T WE LEAVE THEM SOME ROOM TO PLAY...
...BY CHEERING ON THE BOYS?
Y-YOU GUYS! HOW COULD YOU LEAVE ME ALONE WITH NAM-JOO?!!
H-HOLD ON!!
I DON'T WANNA PLAY DODGEBALL EITHER!!
NICE. NOW WE DON'T HAVE TO WORRY ABOUT THE OTHERS, RIGHT?
CHILL OUT, GEEZ!
HEH!

C'MON, WE'RE S'POSED TO RUN AND SWEAT IN GYM.
CHEERING FOR THE BOYS? WHAT A WASTE...
TCH!
......
DON'T TELL ME YOU WANNA CHEER FOR WHIE-YOUNG TOO?
WH-WHAT ARE YOU TALKING ABOUT? WHY WHIE-YOUNG?!
TODAY I WATCHED YOU STARING AT HIM IN CLASS.
...WHEN YOU RAN OUT AT LUNCH YESTERDAY AND CAME BACK ALL WET...
...WASN'T THAT ABOUT HIM?
HONESTLY, I THINK IT'D BE BETTER TO AVOID A GUY LIKE HIM.
BUT IF YOU'RE ALREADY INTO HIM, THERE'S NOTHING I CAN DO.
BESIDES, IN MY EYES...
HEY GUYS! OVER THERE. IT LOOKS LIKE THE GIRLS ARE GONNA CHEER FOR US. WE HAFTA WIN!
I HATE RUNNING. I'LL BE IN GOAL.
GOAL-KEEPER? JUST BE A STRIKER!
NO, I AM.
I'M THE GOAL-KEEPER, MAN.

NO, LET ME BE GOALKEEPER.
JUST STAND IN FRONT OF A GOAL-POST AND SHOOT THE BALL PAST IT. YOU'RE GOOD AT THAT!
...HE'S ALREADY MAJORLY INTERESTED IN YOU.
WH-WHAT?! CONFESS?! I THINK YOU'VE MISUNDER-STOOD SOMETHING HERE.
IT'S NOT LIKE THAT, OKAY? I'M NOT INTERESTED IN HIM AT ALL...!
IT'S YOUR SPECIALTY. WHAT'S HOLDING YOU BACK?
YOU'VE GOT A GOOD SHOT THIS TIME, SO NO NEED TO WAIT.
CONFESS JUST LIKE YOU USED TO!
I CAN TELL YOU HAVE FEELINGS FOR HIM JUST BY LOOKING YOU IN THE EYE, YA KNOW?
WHAT'S THE MATTER? WHY'RE YOU PRETENDING YOU'RE NOT WHEN YOU OBVIOUSLY ARE? DON'T I KNOW YOU?

I DON'T KNOW HOW LONG IT'S BEEN GOING ON, BUT...
딸랑..
DDALRANG (TWINKLE)
DDALRANG
딸랑..
DDALRANG
딸랑!..
DDALRANG
딸랑..
...YOU'RE ABSOLUTELY INTO HIM. YOUR EYES ARE SHINING AS BRIGHT AS THE STARS.
F...
FOR REAL ?!!!
WHAT'S WRONG WITH YOU?! YOU USED TO BE ALL OVER THIS KINDA STUFF.
NOW PEOPLE WOULD THINK YOU'RE NAIVE!

STEP 40. SAY THAT YOU LIKE ME!!
BACK TO OUTER SPACE...
I......
NOOOOOOOOOOOOOOOOOOOOOOOOOOOOOOOOOOOOOOO...
I'M INTO WHIE-YOUNG JANG?!!!
NOW LET'S FINISH THE MATCH!!!
OH, CLASS REP! YOU HAVEN'T GONE TO CHEER THE BOYS.
C-CAN I REF?
THANKS!
IF THAT'S TRUE, SINCE WHEN?

...'COS WE KISSED...?
DOOGUN (BADUM)
IS IT...
DOES THAT MEAN I HAVE FEELINGS FOR HIM JUST 'COS OF THE KISS? JUST LIKE THAT?
THE TYPE WHO FALLS FOR PEOPLE EASILY ANYWAY
WHAT'RE YOU DOING, HEE-SO?! FOCUS, YA HEAR?!!
...IT'S FOR THE SECOND TIME. HOW CAN I FALL IN LOVE WITH THE SAME PERSON TWICE...?
IF I REALLY DO LIKE HIM...
FWEEET!
BITLE (REEL)
"HEE-SO EUN VS. NAM-JOO YEO"—THE FINAL MATCH HAS BEGUN!!

삐익
BBIIIK (BEEP)
START!!
탁
TAK (GRAB)
HUP!!
...HEE-SO, ARE YOU NOT GONNA TAKE THIS SERIOUSLY?
ARE YOU MAKING LIGHT OF THIS MATCH?!!
THE TYPE WHO PUTS THE GAME FIRST
MUNG (DAZE)
멍~
FINE. IF YOU WON'T...
...HOW 'BOUT I MAKE YOU?
SHARP BLADE OF THE GREAT ARENA THAT CUTS EVEN SOULS, HEAR MY CALL AND EXTIN-GUISH MY ENEMY!
PAJIJIK (BZZT)

EH?!
SHUAK (WHOOSH)
YOU MEANIE! WHAT THE HELL?!
AXE SHOT!!
!!
TEUUK (GRAB)

SHUUWOO (FSSSHH)
...HE STOPPED MY AXE SHOT WITH ONE HAND...
WHAT'S THIS COMIC BOOK ABOUT AGAIN...?
DOOGUN (BADUM)
두근
WHIE-YOUNG...
AH, THEY WON'T LET ME PLAY GOALIE.
AREN'T YOU PLAYING SOCCER?!!
WH-WHIEEEEK ...!!
AFRAID OF WHIE-YOUNG FOR SOME REASON
WH-WHIE-YOUNG JANG!
WHAT'RE YOU DOING HERE?!!
DUL (SHAKE)
DUL
덜덜
I HATE RUNNING OR KICKING THE BALL...
...SO I THOUGHT DODGE-BALL WOULD BE BETTER...

ANYWAY, WHAT'RE YOU DOING THROWING SOMETHING LIKE THIS AROUND? YOU COULD KILL SOMEONE.
AND YOU GOT IT WITH ONE HAND, YA JERK...!!
HA... HA-HA! I GOT A GOOD ARM!
HIS HAND'S STINGING...
E-EXCUSE ME...
THANKS FOR HELPING ME...
HELPING YOU?
I JUST CAME TO PLAY DODGE-BALL.
OKAY, I'LL BE CAREFUL.
THANKS FOR YOUR CONCERN.
WHY'RE YOU STANDING AROUND IN A DAZE? IF THE BALL HITS YOU IN THE HEAD, IT'LL JUST MAKE YOU STUUUPIDER!
......
WHAT THE HELL, AREN'T YOU GONNA YELL BACK AT ME?
......
WASN'T I JUST PRETTY SARCASTIC?

DOOGUN (BADUM)
AH, I SEE...
BBANHEE (STARE)
빤히~
DOOGUN
MY HEART RACES WHEN I SEE HIS FACE...
......
? ?
THE HELL D'YOU THINK YER LOOKIN' AT? YOU GOT A PROBLEM WITH ME, HUH?
N-NO! SORRY IF I MADE YOU FEEL WEIRD.
...OH-HOH~!
THERE IT IS. THE "FOR-MY-GUY'S-EYES-ONLY" PERSONALITY.
WHY ARE YOU APOLOGIZING? WHAT'S WRONG WITH YOU?

DID YA KNOW, HEE-SO DOES A TOTAL 180 IN FRONT OF A PERSON SHE LIKES?
WHIE-YOUNG JANG. WANNA HEAR SOMETHING INTERESTING?
WHAT?
NAM-JOO!!
AND THE ONE SHE LIKES RIGHT NOW IS...
TUK (SNATCH)
TH-THIS IS ...!!
BLAZING ROAR THAT SHATTERS THE SUN, PHOENIX THAT BURSTS INTO FLAME! LEND ME YOUR POWER!!
WHAT'RE YOU UP TO NOW?

MEGA BLAZE SHOT!!
WHAT?! MEGA?!!
IS THIS SOME KIND OF PERFORMANCE ART ...?
퍽
PUUK (THWACK)
SHE'S GONE BEYOND HER LIMIT AND POWERED UP—
THOUGH YOU WERE MY ENEMY, THAT WAS AMAZING, HEE-SO! THE VICTORY IS ALL YOURS...
척
CHUK (TMP)
You win
WHOOOA—! NOT BAD.
YOU WON WITH JUST ONE THROW.

THANKS FOR THE COMPLIMENT.
...!
C-COMPLIMENT... I MEANT IT MORE LIKE IT'S GOOD YOU HAVE AT LEAST ONE THING YOU'RE GOOD AT.
KOOMTLE (TWITCH)
HOW COULD YOU GO ON LIVING WITHOUT A SINGLE SKILL TO YOUR NAME!!
...THAT KINDA THING!
WHAT THE HELL IS UP WITH YOU?!!
YOU'VE TURNED ALL WEIRD LIKE SOMETHING'S COME OVER YOU!
WHAT'S COME OVER HER IS AN AIR OF INNOCENCE.
AS MEEK AS A LAMB ALL OF A SUDDEN
...OH YEAH. THAT'S GOOD TO KNOW. THANK YOU FOR POINTING IT OUT.
TEE HEE HEE...

OF COURSE, HER BEHAVIOR DEPENDS ON WHO SHE'S WITH, BUT...
...IN FRONT OF A BOY SHE LIKES...
...HEE-SO EUN CHANGES HER PERSONALITY AND THE WAY SHE TALKS.
UMM...
IF YOU DON'T LIKE SOMETHING ABOUT ME, JUST TELL ME.
I-I'LL TRY TO FIX IT.
FIX WHAT? JUST LIVE WITH WHAT YOU'VE GOT.
WHAT'S WRONG WITH YOUR TONGUE? DID YOU BITE IT ...?
WHIE-YOUNG, WHO'S NEVER EXPERIENCED THIS SIDE OF HER...
...IS VERY CONFUSED.

......;;
......
WHOA, DID HEE-SO GET WEIRD.
YOU GOT ANY INSIGHT INTO THAT FOR ME?
I-I'M SORRY, SIR!!
YOU'RE WEIRD TOO!! WHY'RE YOU FOLLOWING ME AROUND AND STARING AT ME?
WHAT'S WRONG WITH YOU GUYS?! ARE YOU ON DRUGS OR SOME-THING?!!

UM...
SOMETHING'S ON YOUR MIND, ISN'T IT?
WHY DON'T YOU COME OUT WITH IT ALREADY, HUH?
GO ON THEN, WHAT IS IT?
MASTER, I OVERHEARD SOMETHING SCARY.
IS IT TRUE THAT YOUR LIFE GETS SHORTER EVERY TIME YOU USE IT?
IS IT TRUE THAT YOUR POWER IS LINKED TO YOUR LIFE?

THEN...
I...
I INVITED HEE-SO TO COME OVER THIS WEEKEND...
...TO SHOW HER THE FLOWERS IN THE GARDEN—
SO WHAT?
SINCE WHEN DOES SHE NEED PERMISSION TO COME HERE?
YOU DON'T HAVE TO REPORT EVERY LITTLE THING TO ME, YOU KNOW?
...IS MY EXISTENCE...
S-SORRY TO BOTHER YOU, SIR...

...HURTING YOU,
MASTER...?

SOMETHING'S BURNING?
WHO'S BURNING WHAT?
WHO'S IN THE KITCHEN?

!!
WHIE-YOUNG!
YOU'RE FINALLY UP?
ARE YOU HUNGRY? I'LL MAKE SOMETHING DELICIOUS. IT'LL JUST TAKE A MINUTE.

...WHAT THE...
BEATRICE SAID YOU'D WAKE UP AROUND NOON, BUT...
...YOU CAME DOWN EARLY.
DULSSUK (BOIL)
들썩
DULSSUK
들썩
BURNING...
HMM...?
IT'S BURNING, YOU IDIOT !!!
EHHH ?!!
IS YOUR NOSE CLOGGED? THE WHOLE HOUSE REEKS OF BURNT FOOD...
...AND YOU DIDN'T NOTICE ?!!
CHIIK (SHIIIII)

A FLASHBACK FROM EARLIER THIS MORNING♥
IT'S SO EARLY... DO YOU EVEN KNOW WHAT TIME IT IS?
ANYWAY, HOW COME YOU'RE COOKING IN MY KITCHEN?
THE TIME IS 8 A.M.
BEATRICE WENT OFF EARLY WITH YOUR GRANDMA, SO I JUST...;;
I'M TRAUMATIZED JUST FROM HEARING THE NAME.
I WAS BUSY MAKING PANCAKE BATTER. AHH, I CAN'T BELIEVE MY SPECIAL "SWEET-AND-SOUR FUSION BOILED EGG WITH HAM, TUNA, AND MAYONNAISE" HAS TURNED TO ASH...
NAKSIM (DROOP)
H-HEE-SO! WHAT BRINGS YOU HERE AT THIS HOUR?
WILL THAT BE OKAY? WELL, SHE'S A GOOD COOK...
DON'T WORRY! I'LL MAKE BREAKFAST!!
YES!
...SO I WAS ABOUT TO GO WITH HER TO PICK THEM UP. WE'LL BE BACK BY NINE.
GRANDMA'S FRIEND HAS COME TO SEOUL WITH SOME FRUITS AND VEGETABLES...
YOU'VE COME VERY EARLY, DEAR.
HEE-SO EUN ARRIVED AT 7 A.M.!
Y-YES, BUT...
...I DIDN'T EXPECT YOU THIS EARLY SINCE IT'S SUNDAY. I THOUGHT YOU'D BE HERE AROUND LUNCH...
YOU SAID TO COME OVER TODAY. 'COS YOU HAD SOMETHING TO SHOW ME.
......
AND THAT'S HOW IT HAPPENED.

HOW COME YOU'RE UP EARLY? YOU USUALLY SLEEP A LOT.
GUIYUM
GUIYUM (CUTE)
귀엽귀엽
GYAWOOT (TILT)
갸웃..
YOU HAVEN'T BEEN SLEEPING AT SCHOOL EITHER. HAVE YOU DECIDED TO BE A GOOD BOY?
......
WHY ARE YOU TALKING ALL CUTESY? IT'S GROSS.
......
AND IT'S NONE OF YOUR BUSINESS.
WE HAVE RICE, DON'T WE?
I'M HUNGRY.
OH! W-WE'LL HAVE TO MAKE NEW RICE 'COS ATE ALL O WHAT WAS LEFT...
I CAME HERE WITHOUT BREAKFAST SO...
...SO YOU'VE COME HERE TO BE A MOOCHER.
N-NO! HANG ON!
WE'VE GOT THIS! HEE-SO EUN'S SPECIAL "CHOCOLATE MAYONNAISE SEAFOOD PANCAKES"!
CHOCOLATE... MAYONNAISE...?
THE BATTER'S READY. I JUST NEED TO FRY THEM UP! ♥
HEE-SO EUN'S SPECIAL "YOGURT JELLY NOODLES"!!
WHY'RE YOU DOING ALL THIS? DO YOU WANT SOMETHING FROM ME?
DON'T. I'LL EAT NOODLES.
NOODLES?
LET ME BOIL THEM FOR YOU!!
I SAID DON'T! I JUST WANNA EAT NORMAL FOOD!!
IF THAT'S THE CASE, CUT THE CRAP AND GET TO THE POINT!!
WOO (POUT)

NOW PLEASE ENJOY YOUR MEAL.
......
SANGLE (SMILE)
생글
SANGLE
생글
HERE, KIMCHI! KIMCHI IS ESSENTIAL TO SAVORING NOODLES~! ♥
CHUK (TAK)
척
IT'S KIMCHI...
MADE HIS OWN NOODLES
W-WAIT!!
...YOU... WHY ARE YOU DOING THIS?
WELL, I HEARD FROM BEATRICE.
...HEARD? ABOUT WHAT?
ABOUT THE FLOWERS IN THE GARDEN.
BEATRICE SAID...
...HE WANTED TO SHOW ME THE FLOWERS AND THEN...
...HE SAID THAT YOU MADE THEM BLOOM.
I'M TOUCHED.
HE SAID YOU DID IT?
YOU'VE... ALL TOTALLY MISUNDERSTOOD SOMETHING.

...WHY'D YOU COME HERE...
...LOOKING SO RIDIC-ULOUS?
ANYWAY...
SORRY TO DISAPPOINT YOU, BUT...
...I DON'T HAVE TIME FOR THAT KIND OF POINTLESS CRAP.
AND THE SMELL!! YOUR PERFUME'S SO STRONG, YOU COULDN'T EVEN SMELL THE FOOD BURNING!
(PRODUCTS SHE'S WEARING) —HOT PINK LIP GLOSS —ORANGE-SCENTED PERFUME
YOU KEEP UP WITH THAT BABY TALK...
...WHICH ANNOYS ME.
AND...
...YOUR LIPS ARE ALL GREASY.
NOT TO MENTION YOU'VE RUN WILD IN MY KITCHEN MAKING YOUR NASTY DISHES.
HUH...?

I HAVE NO IDEA WHY YOU'RE DOING THIS WHEN IT DOESN'T SUIT YOU AT ALL.
ACTING LIKE YOU'RE PRETTY AND NICE ISN'T GOING TO GET YOU ANYWHERE.
YOU SHOULD THINK ABOUT HOW MUCH HARM YOU'RE DOING...
TALK ABOUT IDIOTIC.
NAHEU (SHOCK)
UN-SPEAKABLE CHARMS...
...ACTING COY...
...AND UN-BELIEVABLE COOKING.
ARGH!!!

YEAH, YOU'RE DAMN RIGHT. I'VE BEEN ACTING LIKE I'M PRETTY AND NICE! SO WHAT?!
I'VE BEEN COY AND CHARMING, SO WHAT?!!
CAN'T YOU JUST SAY "YOU LOOK PRETTY TODAY" OR "YOU'RE SO NICE"? THAT'S WHAT PEOPLE SAY EVEN IF THEY DON'T REALLY MEAN IT, YOU TOTALLY ROTTEN BASTARD!!!
SSIGUN (MIFF)
SSIGUN
SSIGUN
KRUNG (ROAR)
THERE...
...THAT'S MORE LIKE IT.
SEE? IT'S BETTER BEING YOURSELF.
MUCH BETTER.
PFFT!
......
GRRRRARRGH!
IS THAT REALLY WHAT YOU THINK OF ME...
ISN'T IT ALSO ME... IF I'M BEING CUTE?

WHAT...?
IF YOU PREFER ROUGH, I CAN DO ROUGH.
THIS IS ME, ISN'T IT?
I NEED SOME AIR.
YOU KEEP SNARFING DOWN THOSE NOODLES!
WHERE ARE YOU GOING?
HAAAAH...
I HATE HIM, BUT...
...HOW COME I LIKE HIM SO MUCH?
HAVING HER SPECIAL CUTE AND CHARMING ACT REJECTED...
HAAAH...
...WAS QUITE SHOCKING TO HEE-SO.
IT HAD ALWAYS WORKED TILL NOW...

AHH, I WISH...
...I COULD TELL EVERYTHING TO BEATRICE AND FEEL BETTER...
WHAT IN THE WORLD...
...DID I GET UP SO EARLY FOR?
AND...
...SHE'D GOTTEN UP IN THE VERY EARLY MORNING TO PUT ON MAKE-UP TOO...
...BUT I CAN'T DO THAT ANYMORE.
WHAT'S WRONG WITH ME...?
HAAAAH...
WHY ARE YOU SIGHING?
BEATRICE TOLD ME HE LIKES ME...
...SO I DECIDED TO PROTECT HIS HEART...
IT'S ONLY BEEN A FEW DAYS SINCE, AND I'VE TURNED INTO THIS.

I'M BACK, HEE-SO.
WE'VE GOT PERSIMMONS, PEPPERS, SWEET POTATOES, GARLIC, BEANS, CHESTNUTS, SESAME OIL, AND...
D-DID YOU CARRY THEM ALL BY YOURSELF? WHAT ABOUT GRANDMA?!!
DDUK (GAPE)
떡
B-BEATRICE!! WHAT IS ALL THAT?!
I LEFT HER WITH HER FRIEND.
BUT HOW COULD SHE LET YOU CARRY ALL THAT?!
...OMIGOSH, YOU LOOK LIKE THE WEAKEST PERSON ON EARTH. WHERE IS ALL THAT STRENGTH COMING FROM...?
I DIDN'T REALIZE HOW STRONG I AM.
I WASN'T SURE IF I COULD AT FIRST EITHER, BUT THEY WERE LIGHT AS A FEATHER.
HUT!!

ACHOO!
HAVE YOU CAUGHT A COLD, HEE-SO?
HUH?
N-NO, NO, IT'S JUST...
HOLD ON...
DON'T TELL ME YOU CAME HERE LIKE THAT?
IT'S ALMOST NOVEMBER! HOW CAN YOU BE OUTSIDE IN JUST THAT?!
WHAT?
I CAN TAKE THE COLD.
NYEE-HEE!
IS THAT PERFUME?
KUNG (SNIFF) KUNG
BOOTS, BELT, AND ACCES-SORIES! AREN'T THEY HEE-JOO'S?
WHAT IS ALL THIS!
AND THE MAKE-UP...
I-I BORROWED THEM.
YOU'VE EVEN GOT GOOSE BUMPS ON YOUR ARMS!!
ARE YOU OUT OF YOUR MIND?!!
HEE-JOO WILL KILL YOU IF YOU GET CAUGHT!!
...EH...?

WOW, YOUR HAIR...
IT MUST HAVE TAKEN QUITE SOME TIME...
...TO BLOW-DRY IT.
ABOUT THIRTY MINUTES...
HOW EARLY DID YOU GET UP TO DO ALL THIS?
UMM... AROUND SIX...?
IT MEANS YOU HAVE SOMEONE...
...YOU WANT TO LOOK PRETTY FOR.
IT'S...
...NOT ME, IS IT?
......
ACTUALLY IT'S...

...YOU ASKED ME...
...TO CONFESS TO YOU OUT LOUD...
...AND YOU MADE ME THINK THERE WAS HOPE...
I DIDN'T EXPECT THIS EITHER.
I WAS LIKE, "HUH? WHAT'S WRONG WITH ME?" AND THEN...
..."DO I LIKE HIM?" AND THEN...
...EVER SINCE I REALIZED I DO, I CAN'T CONTROL MYSELF...
WHAT?!
MY MASTER?!!
...WHO?
......
LOOK, BEATRICE.
I MUST BE A HOPELESS IDIOT.
SO YOU MEAN THAT NO MATTER WHAT...
...I CAN'T BE YOUR BOYFRIEND.
IT'S NOT THE SAME THING! FOR YOU...
...IT'S SOMETHING MORE COMPLICATED AND PURE, NOT RAW EMOTION LIKE THIS...

WHEN I WAS SEPARATED FROM WON-JUN...
...I DECIDED TO NOT GIVE UP MY HEART SO EASILY ANYMORE.
I WAS DETERMINED TO BE STRONG AND NOT BE RULED BY MY EMOTIONS OR THE FEELINGS OF THE MOMENT. BUT LOOK AT ME NOW.
I'M DOING IT AGAIN. NOTHING'S CHANGED.
I GET ENTRANCED AT THE DROP OF A HAT...
...I LIKE HIM RIGHT AWAY...
...I BECOME PASSIONATE IN A SECOND...
...AND FALL MADLY IN LOVE WITH HIM LIKE A FOOL.
AS QUICKLY AS I START...
...I FEEL LIKE I CAN SEE THE END JUST AS FAST.

WHEN I'M INTO SOME-THING, I SPEND LIKE I'M ON FIRE AND THEN LOOK AROUND FOR THE NEXT BIG THING...
IT'S KIND OF LIKE IMPULSE BUYING.
WILL I TURN OUT LIKE HEE-JOO?
RELATION-SHIPS MIGHT BE...
...GETTING MORE AND MORE CASUAL FOR ME.
WHAT DO YOU MEAN YOU CAN SEE THE END?
......
I MEAN THAT IT WON'T LAST LONG.
WHAT?! YOU SHOULDN'T BE THINKING SUCH TWISTED THINGS, HEE-SO!!
YOU SHOULD BE MATURING AS YOU GAIN EXPERIENCE!!
BUT NO MATTER HOW MUCH I THINK ABOUT IT...
...IT ALWAYS TURNS OUT THE SAME.

......
IF I LIKE HIM, I CONFESS AND TIE MYSELF TO HIM...
...THEN I GO OUT WITH HIM, AND THEN IT ENDS.
TO NY
EVEN THOUGH I LIKE HIM NOW...
...WHEN I THINK ABOUT HOW IT'LL END AT SOME POINT, I CAN'T HELP FEELING GLOOMY.
SHE HAS PRETENDED TO BE FINE SO FAR, BUT...
...SHE'S BEEN HURT EVERY TIME.
THERE IS ONE HEART THAT WOULD STAY UNCHANGING, ETERNAL, AND TRUE...
...A HEART THAT WOULD LOVE ONLY YOU...
...HEE-SO.
IF THERE WAS SOMEONE...
...HEE-SO COULD TRUST ABSOLUTELY...
OHH~! REALLY?
WHERE?

IF ANYONE CAN...
...LOVE HER ENOUGH...
HEE-HEE...
헤헷~

...TO ERASE THOSE MEMORIES...

Y-YOU IDIOT.
WHEN YOU SAY SOMETHING LIKE THAT, IT JUST MAKES ME FEEL GUILTY.

HEE-SO...

...YOU DON'T NEED TO FEEL SORRY FOR ME.

......
YOU MEAN I SHOULD LET WHIE-YOUNG DUMP ME?
HA-HA, I WOULDN'T DARE...
TONY
EVEN THOUGH I CAME LOOKING ALL CUTE AND EVERYTHING...
...HE COULDN'T CARE LESS. DAMMIT...
H-HE MIGHT FEEL DIFFERENT INSIDE—
I KNOW THAT IT CAN'T BE ME...
DON'T HESITATE. JUST DO WHAT YOU HAVE TO DO. CONFESS AND TIE YOURSELF TO HIM NICE AND TIGHT.
INSTEAD, I THINK IT'S A GOOD THING.
...BUT...
DON'T WORRY, HEE-SO.
I WILL ALWAYS BE ON YOUR SIDE.
I WANT...
...WHATEVER YOU WANT.

DO YOUR BEST FAITHFULLY, JUST LIKE ALWAYS.
I'LL HELP YOU THIS TIME.
...THE FEELINGS I HAVE...
AND I HOPE FOR YOUR SAKE THAT THIS LOVE IS HERE TO STAY.
...ARE DEFINITELY THE REAL THING.
...THANK YOU...
...BEATRICE.
DON'T BE.
YOU'LL BE STRONG LIKE I SAID, WON'T YOU?
......
...YOU'RE ENCOURAG-ING ME.
I FEEL ASHAMED.

AND...
...THE FEELINGS THAT I HAVE ARE REALLY HIS.
...WHAT IS IT?
HAVE SOME PERSIMMONS. THEY'RE FROM GRANDMA'S FRIEND.
...MASTER.
I HEARD YOU WERE MEAN TO HEE-SO TODAY?
SAGAK (PEEL)
사각
SAGAK
사각

YOU WERE BAD, MASTER.
YOU SHOULDN' IGNORE SOMEBODY'S SINCERITY.
SHE WAS DOING CRAZY STUFF! SHE WAS A BIG PAIN IN THE ASS!!
IF I'D EATEN THAT FOOD SHE MADE, I'DVE BEEN DEAD FOR SURE!!
SAGAK (PEEL)
사각
SAGAK :
사각 :
WHAT ARE YOU TALKING ABOUT?
SHE JUST WANTED TO LOOK PRETTY FOR YOU...
...AND SHE PUT IN A LOT OF EFFORT.

...YOU SHOULD HAVE NOTICED IT BY NOW...
YOU'RE SLOWER THAN I EXPECTED, MASTER.
THAT'S ENOUGH, YOU JERK!!
HERE YOU GO, SIR.
A PAIN IN THE ASS? SHE LOOKED NICE WITH THE LIP GLOSS, FASHIONABLE CLOTHES, AND PRETTY HAIR.
WOULDN'T YOU SAY SHE WAS "EASY ON THE EYES"?
TO-NI

......
WHY'RE YOU JUMPING DOWN MY THROAT?
IT'D BE NICE IF YOU KNEW...
...EVEN WITHOUT HER TELLING YOU...
THEY DON'T THINK ABOUT THE CONSEQUENCES.
THEY OVER-LOOK THE DELICATE HEARTS OF WOMEN.
HEY—
HEY!
THIS IS WHY MEN ARE TROUBLE-SOME.
WHY THE HELL WOULD YOU BE DISAPPOINTED!!
I'M DISAPPOINTED THAT YOU'RE NO DIFFERENT.

YOU SHOULD TAKE RESPONSIBILITY LIKE A MAN.
DO?
NOW...
...WHAT ARE YOU GOING TO DO ABOUT HEE-SO?
......
...A BOY NEVER KISSES A GIRL WITHOUT REASON, RIGHT?
UNLESS WE'RE TALKING ABOUT A DAMNED JERK...
......
D-DAMNED JERK...?
WHAT THE HELL ARE YOU GOING ON ABOUT?
RESPONSIBILITY FOR WHAT?
IT WOULD BE A GOOD IDEA FOR YOU...
...TO REFLECT ON YOUR ACTIONS...
YOU KISSED HEE-SO.
I'VE HEARD ALL ABOUT IT.

WHENEVER I'VE ASKED YOU HOW YOU FEEL ABOUT HEE-SO...
...YOU'VE PLAYED DUMB.
LET ME EAT...MY...
BUT NOT KNOWING ISN'T AN ANSWER.
EITHER YOU'RE NOT SURE OR YOU'RE AVOIDING IT ON PURPOSE.
MASTER, I HAVE BEEN WATCHING...
...PERSIMMON...
...YOU ACT INDIFFERENT TO HEE-SO.
BUT YOU'RE NOT.
I KNOW THAT BECAUSE ABOVE ALL THINGS, YOU GAVE ME A HEART WITH A PURPOSE, MASTER.

SO I THINK THAT WHAT I FEEL FOR HEE-SO—
UNEATEN PERSIMMON...
A HEART WITH A WISH...
...TO PROTECT A PRECIOUS PERSON.
AND BECAUSE OF THAT WISH...
...I HAVE EYES FOR NO ONE BUT HER.
I'M LIKE THIS BECAUSE THE HEART THAT WAS GIVEN TO ME WAS ONLY EVER "FOR HEE-SO EUN."

IF THE PROBLEM IS THAT YOUR FEELINGS FOR HEE-SO ARE UNCERTAIN...
...THEN PERHAPS THAT MIGHT BE MY FAULT.
SO IF I WAS TO RETURN THE HEART I RECEIVED FROM YOU—
IT ALL COMES FROM YOU, MASTER.

AND EVEN IF YOU'RE RIGHT...
...IT'S ALL ANCIENT HISTORY NOW.
I DON'T WANNA HEAR ANOTHER WORD!
CHANGKANG (CLATTER)
챙강!
HE DIDN'T GET TO EAT ANY OF IT IN THE END... ㅠㅅㅠ
IF I LOST SOMETHING 'COS OF YOU, IT WAS JUST THE EMOTIONS FROM THAT CHILDHOOD MOMENT.
THEY DON'T HAVE ANY INFLUENCE OVER ME NOW.
AND AS FOR THAT KISS...
...THAT WAS JUST 'COS WE...
...GOT CARRIED AWAY BY THE MOO AND ALL.
BUT...

DAMMIT...
THAT'S JUST WHAT MEN DO!
BUT...
BUT...
I MEAN, IT WAS RAINING...
...AND WE WERE THERE, JUST THE TWO OF US...
...AND IT JUST HAPPENED.

IS IT TRUE THAT YOU RISK YOUR LIFE EVERY TIME YOU USE YOUR POWERS?
WHAT ON EARTH POSSESSED YOU TO GIVE YOUR HEART TO ME?!

......
IF THAT'S TRUE...
...WHAT ABOUT MY EXISTENCE?
...WHAT THE—
WHERE'D YOU HEAR THAT?
I'VE BEEN THINKING ABOUT HOW TO RETURN YOUR GENEROSITY...
...BUT IF MY VERY EXISTENCE IS LIKE POISON TO YOU...
IF I GIVE BACK WHAT I RECEIVED...
...WOULD THAT BRING YOUR LIFE BACK, EVEN A LITTLE?
......

WOULD IT...
...MAKE YOU DISAPPEAR?
DAMN...
YOU NEVER STOP WHINING ABOUT THAT HEART...
IF I TAKE IT BACK LIKE YOU SAID...
...WHAT HAPPENS TO YOU?

Y-YOU WOULDN'T?
WHERE'D YOU GET THAT IDEA?
KOOMTLE (TWITCH)
꿈틀..
FIND...
...THE HEART YOU LOST...
ANYWAY, IT MAKES NO DIFFERENCE.
YOU'VE TALKED ABOUT RETURNING THAT HEART. HOW'RE YOU GONNA DO THAT? IN A BASKET?
NOT TO MENTION, YOU MAKE IT SOUND LIKE I'D CHANGE IF I GOT IT BACK.
TONY

YOU SERIOUSLY BUY INTO THAT CRAP?!!
UGH, I'LL TAKE CARE OF MYSELF, THANK YOU VERY MUCH!!
M-MASTER ...!!
I KNOW THAT MORE THAN ANYTHING...
...IF HE DISAPPEARS...
...IT'LL BREAK HER HEART INTO A THOUSAND PIECES...
ALL RIGHT, LET'S BE THE BEST THAT HEE-SO EUN CAN BE!
WHATEVER I FEEL FOR HEE-SO...
LET'S FACE THAT WHIE-YOUNG JANG WITH COURAGE TOMORROW!!

PLEASE WAIT, MASTER!
I HAVE SOMETHING TO GIVE YOU!!
...I HATE NOTHING MORE THAN SEEING HER CRY.
WHAT NOW?
HE'S ALWAYS...

I'LL GIVE THIS TO YOU.
PLEASE ACCEPT IT, SIR.
THIS...
SSK (SHK)
......
NOW HERE!!
POOK (SHOVE)
DON'T FUSS, MASTER. JUST TAKE IT.
ISN'T THAT THE DOG COLLAR HEE-SO PUT ON YOU?!
WHAT THE HECK AM I S'POSED TO DO WITH IT?!!

...HEE-SO LIKES.
SHE WILL BE STARTING FOR REAL TODAY, SO DON'T BE MEAN.
THAT IS A LUXURY RESERVED FOR THE ONE...
I WANT TO HEAR GOOD NEWS. HAVE A GOOD DAY, MASTER—
BE CAREFUL OF CARS NOW-!
WHAT IS HE TALKING ABOUT?

STEP 41. HEE-SO, FLYING
<ANNOUNCEMENT FROM THE CLASS REP> PLEASE HAND IN YOUR COMPOSITION ASSIGNMENT—
E-EXCUSE ME...YOUR H-HOMEWORK, PLEASE...
CLASS REP
H-HE'S SCARY!

I DON'T HAVE IT. YOU KNOW THAT...
B-BECAUSE I-I'M THE CLASS REP...
...SO WHY D'YOU KEEP ASKING ME?
IT'S A PAIN IN THE BUTT.
A-ANYONE WHO DIDN'T DO THEIR WORK...
HIS EYES... THEY CHILL ME TO THE BONE!!
덜덜덜
DUL DUL DUL (SHAKE)
...NEEDS TO GIVE A REASON...
JUST SAY I'M SICK. I'VE GOT A COLD OR SOMETHING.
WHAT A WEIRD CHICK...
SICK?!
HAVE YOU CAUGHT A COLD, WHIE-YOUNG?!!
......
WHAT WAS THAT?!
깜짝
KAMJJACK (JUMP)

CHUK (TAK)
DO YOU HAVE A FEVER?
TANG (BANG)
WHAT'S YOUR DEAL?!!
YOU'RE VULNERABLE TO COLD, SO YOU SHOULD'VE BEEN MORE CAREFUL.
UMM... I CAN'T TELL WHETHER YOU HAVE A FEVER OR NOT.
WHAT THE HELL?! TAKE YOUR HAND OFF RIGHT NOW, YA HEAR ME?!!

SO LIKE I SAID, I DON'T ...!!
OH, YEAH...
...THIS MIGHT HELP ME FIGURE IT OUT, RIGHT?
......
DUMMY...
...I'M CHECKING TO SEE IF YOU HAVE A FEVER.
...HEY, YOU...
...WHAT ARE YOU DOING?

WHY IS SHE STARING AT ME?
뚜 DO 뚜 DO 뚜 DO 뚜 DO 뚜 DO
DO (BEEP)
WHAT IS ALL THIS?!
우르르 WOORRR (FWSH)
PAINKILLER
DIARRHEA
BIRTH CONTROL
COLD & FLU
NEVER MIND THAT...
I SAID I'M NOT SICK!!
...WHAT THE HELL IS ALL THIS?
...I BROUGHT EVERYTHING THEY HAD AT THE NURSE'S OFFICE.
YOU LOOKED BAD DURING CLASS. BUT SINCE I DON'T KNOW WHAT'S WRONG...
I RAN AS FAST AS I COULD.
헉 HFF!
헉 HFF!
BIRTH CONTROL?!!
수북 PILED UP...
WHAT'S WITH HER?
......

DDAK (PSSHT)
HERE...
...I BOUGHT YOU A SODA TO TAKE IT WITH. CHOOSE ONE.
CHWAAAK (FWSHHHT)
DOOK (DRIP)
DOOK
OOPS, DARN!! IT MUST'VE GOTTEN SHAKEN UP...WHEN I WAS RUNNING HERE!!
I JUST WANTED IT TO GO DOWN EASY FOR YOU...
WHO TAKES PILLS WITH SODA, YOU IDIOT?!!
NAM-JOO PASSING BY
I-IS IT REALLY NOT OKAY?
TAKE PILLS WITH WATER ~!
SHWAHHH (SPLASH)
DAMMIT. MY CLOTHES AND HAIR ARE ALL STICKY.
WHAT IS SHE THINKING?
THERE'S GOTTA BE SOMETHING BEHIND ALL THIS.

......
WHAT'RE YOU DOING SITTING IN FRONT OF THE MEN'S ROOM?
MEN
AH!
HERE'S A TOWEL!!
OH NOOO~! YOUR SHIRT'S ALL STAINED...;;
......
WHY DON'T YOU TAKE IT OFF? YOU CAN WEAR MY CARDIGAN FOR A WHILE!
IT'S BIG.
UH, HELL NO?!
I HAVE MY GYM STUFF...SO QUIT OVER-REACTING.
THEN AT LEAST GIVE ME THE SHIRT!
I'LL WASH IT FOR YOU!
I SAID NO!!

STAINS ON A WHITE SHIRT HAVE TO BE TAKEN CARE OF RIGHT AWAY.
OTHERWISE THEY'LL NEVER COME OUT.
STOLE AND WASHED IT
......
AT THIS POINT, ALL I REALLY WANT TO KNOW IS WHAT THE HELL IS RUNNING THROUGH YOUR HEAD.
HMM...?
WHAT... ME?
YOUR ATTITUDE TOWARD ME'S TAKEN A COMPLETE 180.
YOU'VE CROSSED THE LINE OF WHAT CAN BE DEEMED ACCEPTABLE.
OH! ISN'T THIS A CHANCE TO CONFESS MY FEELINGS TO HIM NATURALLY?!
TH-THAT'S 'COS... I...

MAYBE IT'S TOO SOON FOR A FULL-ON CONFESSION?
JUST LOOK AT THAT SCOWL.
WHAT?!
MY BEAUTY(?) AND SPECIAL CHARMS HAVEN'T WORKED, AND I'VE SCREWED UP LEFT AND RIGHT...
침울...
CHIMWOOL (GLUM)
OKAY. ONCE I PIQUE HIS INTEREST IN ME...
...I'LL WIN POINTS ONE BY ONE!
HEE-SO EUN BEGINS TO THINK SYSTEMATICALLY.
불끈!
BOOLKUN (CLENCH)
HEY, WHAT'RE YOU PLOTTING WITH THIS PEABRAIN OF YOURS?
SOMETHING ABOUT IT STINKS TO HIGH HEAVEN!
TUK (TAK)
탁
KAMJJAK (STARTLE)

WH-WHAT STINKS?!
IS IT A SIN TO DO MY BEST?!
THERE'S NO REASON FOR YOU TO BE DOING YOUR USELESS BEST.
KOOWOOK (SHOVE)
꾸욱~
WH-WHY DON'T YOU LET GO OF ME FIRST?
WHY IS IT USELESS? IT'LL FIRM UP OUR FRIENDSHIP AND BRING US CLOSER AND...!
AND WHY SHOULD WE GET CLOSER?
WHINGSUL SOOSUL (MEANDER)
S-SO WE'RE OPEN TO EACH OTHER AND CAN GET TO BE BETTER FRIENDS, AND...
AND WHY SHOULD I BE OPEN TO YOU?
THAT'S... THAT'S... 'C-COS ...!!
...I WANT YOU TO LIKE ME!!
BURUK (YELL)
버럭
PULRUK (FLAP)
펄럭

HUH...?
"WHY SHOULD I LIKE YOU?" OR SOME-THING...?
D-DON'T YOU FEEL LIKE PICKING AT WHAT I SAID THIS TIME?
......
CRAP! I WAS TOO DIRECT!!

I-IF YOU'RE DYING TO KNOW, YOU CAN JUST ASK ME.
EVEN IF I'M EMBARRASSED, I'LL TELL YOU.
HA-HA...
...NOT REALLY...
......
...AND I DON'T WANNA HEAR IT.
EH?!
YOU'LL JUST SPOUT NONSENSE...
NONSENSE?! DO YOU HAVE ANY IDEA HOW SERIOUS I AM NOW?! HOW COULD YOU...
WELL...
......
...YOU TRY GETTING DRENCHED WITH SODA.
THEN YOU'LL KNOW HOW HARD IT IS TO SAY NICE THINGS.
I'VE... TOTALLY BECOME HIS PET HATE.

I SHOULD DO SOMETHING TO MAKE IT UP TO HIM...
WAIT A MINUTE, WHIE-YOUNG!
WHAT NOW?
YOUR HAND, GIVE ME YOUR HAND!
DUIJUK (DIG) DUIJUK
뒤적 뒤적!
...THIS IS...
TOODOOK (DROP)
투둑...
WARRRR (CASCADE)
와르르—

THEY COME IN HANDY WHEN YOU FEEL BAD OR TIRED!
SO DON'T GIVE ME THAT LOOK.
HAVE SOME WHENEVER YOU NEED A PICK-ME-UP. IT'S MY EMERGENCY STASH.
......
WHY'RE YOU GIVING ME YOUR STASH?
AIEEE~! YOU DON'T HAVE TO BE TOUCHED. IT'S NOTHING.
I KNOW IT'S NOTHING.
TEE-HEE!
SFX: SALRANG (WIGGLE) SALRANG
IF I GET SOMETHING DELICIOUS...
...I'LL ALWAYS OFFER IT TO YOU FIRST.
...WHAT? YOU...
...WANT ME TO LIKE YOU?

THAT IS A LUXURY RESERVED FOR THE ONE...
...HEE-SO LIKES.
DAMMIT. WHAT THE HELL IS THAT?
SO WHAT...
...WHAT DO YOU WANT ME TO DO?

OHHH, YOU HAVE THIS ONE~!
IT'S THE SAME AS MINE~♥
GIMME, OKAY?
I WON'T HURT IT.
PLEASE? PLEASE? PLEASE?
SHUT UP!
WHY?!
GIVE IT TO ME? C'MON.
RIGHT! YOUR PHONE!!
YOU PUT THE TWO PHONES LIKE THIS...
...AND THEN, AND THEN ...
BIIK (BEEP) BIIK BIIK
DO YOU KNOW ABOUT INFRARED COMMUNICATION?
EVEN THE CLASS REP COULDN'T GET WHIE-YOUNG'S NUMBER, BUT HEE-SO DID!!
THIS IS HOW HEE-SO EUN GETS BOYS' NUMBERS.
NAM-JOO PASSING BY
WHAT DID YOU JUST DO WITHOUT MY SAY-SO?!
GOOD, NETWORK OF EMERGENCY CONTACTS...
...COMPLETE!
Infrared communication complete
Whie-Young Jang 010-XXX-WXYZ

EVER SINCE...
PM 3:48
Check out this dog! What a huge head!
DDIRING (BEEP)
띠링!
PM 3:50
Look at him~! He's peeing on the utility pole. So cute~! >ω<
PM 3:51
Ah! He's gone to his owner. Pooh~! ㅠㅅㅠ
DDIRING
띠링
PM 3:53
Look at the sky~! The clouds look like a flock of sheep~!♥ Do you see it?
PM 3:55
I just twisted my ankle. Owwwwie! ㅠㅅㅠ
PM 3:58
Self-portrait from the perfect angle~!♥♥ Heh-heh-heh!
...YOU'RE DOING ALL THIS CRAP...
SERIOUSLY, WHAT THE HELL!!
PM. 3:45
PHOTO TO CELEBRATE WHIE AND SO'S FIRST TEXT!!♥
PHOTO TO CELEBRATE WHIE AND SO'S FIRST TEXT!!♥
...IT'S ALMOST LIKE I'M GETTING CARPET BOMBED.
......
DDIRING
띠링
I just bought walnut ice cream. Looks delicious, huh?
WHAT IS YOUR PROBLEM, HUH?
WHAT'S WITH YOU? DO YOU ALWAYS HAVE TO GO OVER-BOARD?!
OOH!
우왓!
AH, WHIE-YOUNG! IT'S OUR FIRST PHONE CALL~!! ♥
Did you see the sky? The clouds are so pretty~! >ω<

GO ON, SEND ME ONE MORE STUPID TEXT!
I'LL SMASH YOUR PHONE!!
NOT LISTENING...;;
AH! THE FLOCK OF SHEEP CLOUDS ARE MOVING FAST! A WOLF MUST BE CHASING THEM...!
SHEEP 1 AND SHEEP 2 ARE RACING!
SHEEP 2'S JUST OVERTAKEN SHEEP 1! AND NOW SHEEP 3'S CUTTING IN!!
FLOCK OF SHEEP PLAY-BY-PLAY
빠끗
BBIKUT (TWIST)
이야아아아악!!!
UAARRGHH!!
깜짝
KAMJJAK (STARTLE)
......
HEE-SO EUN...?
OOOOOOOOOUCH...
HEY, WHAT'S WRONG?! HEE-SO!!
...HEE-SO!!

I...I fell... Uuu... Oh no... I......think... ...it...it's broken!! Omigosh! There's bl...! Blood...!!
BROKEN?!! HEY, WHERE ARE YOU NOW?!!
I'LL BE RIGHT THERE...
...SO DON'T MOVE !!
PAAK (DASH)
MY PALM'S SKINNED AND BLOODY...
...WHIE-YOUNG! WHIE-YOUNG JANG? ...WE GOT CUT OFF?
AND MY... PRECIOUS ICE CREAM.
I DIDN'T EVEN GET TO TAKE ONE BITE, AND IT'S BROKEN...
WAAH...
...DIDN'T WHIE-YOUNG...
...JUST SAY HE WAS COMING HERE?
AH! IT'S...

WOW, A KITE ~!
ARE YOU GUYS FLYING KITES? IT LOOKS LIKE FUN ~! ♥
I MADE IT TODAY AT SCHOOL. IT'S NOT AS GOOD AS AN AIRPLANE...
...BUT IT'S OKAY TO PLAY WITH.
YOU MUST BE A RICH KID~!
YOU SOUND LIKE ONE TOO.
HMPH!
CAN I TRY IT JUST ONCE? C'MON, LEMME HAVE A GO, HUH?
NO! OUTTA MY WAY!
HEY, DON'T BE A JERK. DON'T YOU KNOW THE "GROWN-UPS FIRST" RULE?
I SAID NO, SO WHY'RE YOU BUG-GING ME?
HEY! MY BOYFRIEND'S COMING HERE! DO YOU KNOW HOW SCARY HE IS?!
HE'LL DO ANYTHING FOR ME!!

DON'T WORRY! TRUST ME!!
AH HA HA HA HA!
HA HA HA!
DON'T GO THERE!
IT MIGHT GET STUCK IN THE TREES!
I KNEW IT! NOW WHAT'RE YOU GONNA DO?!
...CAN I JUST PULL THE STRING
YOU IDIOT, IT'LL GET TORN TO BITS!!
......
......

OKAY, OKAY! I'LL GO UP AND BRING IT BACK DOWN!
WHAT ARE YOU TALKING ABOUT?! HOW CAN A GIRL GET UP THERE?!
CHALSSAK (CLING)
MY NICKNAME FROM WHEN I WAS A KID WAS "EUN THE MONKEY." I'M AN EXPERT AT CLIMBING ~!
YOU SURE IT WASN'T "EUN THE PEST"...?;;
...ARE YOU SURE?
SHASAK (SHP)
SHASAK
ALMOST THERE!!

AH!
I GOT IT! SEE, I TOLD YOU I'D GET IT!
WOW! YOU'RE AMAZING! YOU'RE THE BEST, SIS!!
WHIE-YOUNG JANG! HERE, OVER HERE!!

WH...
WHAT THE HELL ARE YOU DOING UP THERE?!!
WHAT EXACTLY DID YOU BREAK AGAIN?!
I'LL BE DOWN IN A MINUTE. HOLD ON!!
TAK (TMP)
탁!
WOODUK (CRACK)
I THINK...
WHIECHUNG (WOBBLE)
휘청!
ACK!!
우드드득!
WOODDDDDK (CRASH)

...I'VE...
...BEEN IN THIS SITUATION BEFORE.
S-SIS?!
I WAS RUNNING TO YOU...
I'VE PROBABLY...
...JUST LIKE THIS THEN TOO.

...ALWAYS BEEN...
...RUNNING TO YOU.
SSRR (SHK)
...THINKING THINGS THROUGH.
EH?
DONGSIL (FLOAT)
RUNNING TO YOU WITHOUT EVER...

TH-THIS...
ISN'T THIS LIKE A PRINCE RUSHING IN TO SAVE A PRINCESS IN DANGER?!
I...
I...
I...
I...?

와락
WARAK (HUG)
I WAS SO SCARED~~!
WAAAH~~!!
...BY THE WAY...
...DIDN'T YOU SAY YOU BROKE SOMETHING? HOW COULD YOU GET UP THERE IF...
찰싹
CHALSSAK (CLING)
WAAAH...
...BROKE? IT WAS MY ICE CREAM...
WAAAAAAH...
EX...
EXCUSE ME...
UWAAAAAH
CAN'T YOU SEE I'M HAVING A MOMENT...?
SHOO, SHOO!
...AND YOU ARE?
YOU'RE SO BEING PLAYED, DUDE...

OHHH~! IS HE THE **BOYFRIEND** YOU WERE TELLING ME ABOUT BEFORE?
THE ONE WHO'D DO ANYTHING FOR YOU...?
...HUH? I'D DO WHAT?
SO YOU'RE THE ONE WHO'S WRAPPED AROUND HER LITTLE FINGER...
...AND SO MADLY IN LOVE WITH HER THAT YOU'D RISK YOUR LIFE FOR HER?
......
N-NO, NO, NO, NO!! I DON'T KNOW THIS BOY!
WHAT A BIG MOUTH!!
WHO ARE YOU, KID? HAVE WE MET?
WR-WRAPPE AROUND HER LITTLE FINGER ...?
HEY SIS, YOU'RE REALLY AWESOME AT CLIMBING. IT LOOKED LIKE YOU WERE FLYING!
EH...?
YEAH, THAT'S ME.
YOU GOT A PROBLEM WITH THAT?
FWEEE-WHEEET!
HAVE FUN WITH YOUR BOY TOY~!

......
AREN'T YOU GETTING OFF? HURRY UP, YOU'RE HEAVY.
......
...WHIE-YOUNG JANG.
YEAH.
WHIE-YOUNG JANG.
I CAN'T KEEP IT INSIDE ANYMORE.
YEAH.
WHIE-YOUNG JANG.
YEAH!
WHIE-YOUNG JANG.
I'M ITCHING TO TALK...
YEAH !!!

I LIKE YOU.
...I LIKE YOU SO MUCH.
IF I DON'T BLURT OUT MY FEELINGS...
...I THINK I MIGHT BURST...
PSS (RUSTLE)
파사…

I LIKE YOU...
TAK (TMP)
탁
I... I SAID IT!!
DOOGUN (BADUM)
THERE, I'VE PITCHED HIM THE BALL!!
SWING YOUR BAT, JANG! WILL IT BE A HOME RUN OR AN OUT?!!
BBUL (SWEAT) BBUL
...YOU TOLD ME ABOUT THE CLOUDS LOOKING LIKE A FLOCK OF SHEEP...

THEY TOTALLY DO LOOK LIKE SHEEP, JUST LIKE YOU SAID. HA-HA...
THEY'RE THE SAME AS...
...IN THE PICTURE YOU SENT BEFORE.
E-EEH?
WHAT'S HE TALKING ABOUT...?
DID HE...
......
...JUST...
....
...TUNE ME OUT?!!
SO ANYWAY...
...WHERE'S SHEEP 1?
SHE TOOK OFF A LONG TIME AGO!
YOU SEEM TO BE IGNORANT OF THE WAYS OF SHEEP.
SHE WAS VERY UPSET AND LEFT.
WHY WAS SHE UPSET?
'COS SHEEP 1 CONFESSED TO SHEEP 2, BUT...
...HE IGNOR HER.
ISN'T HE THE WORST?
......

BURUK (YELL)
I'M NOT DUMPING YOU!!
IF YOU'RE GONNA DUMP ME, DO IT RIGHT!!
SO I CAN DECIDE WHETHER TO BE MAD OR TO TRY HARDER!!
TEMPER, TEMPER.
......
...WHAT? YOU'RE NOT?
THEN...
"SHE'S MINE." "THIS IS MY GIRL."
WHY CAN'T YOU SAY IT?!!
WHY DIDN'T YOU SAY SO?
DO YOU LIKE ME TOO?
......
I REALLY HAD NO IDEA...
...I'D FEEL LIKE THIS...
...I DIDN'T KNOW.
......

I DIDN'T EXPECT...
...THAT I'D BE THIS HAPPY TO HEAR...
...YOUR CONFESSION...
WHY DO YOU KEEP AVOIDING THE SUBJECT?! DAMN YOU!!
...LATELY I HAVEN'T SLEPT MUCH.
SO MY BRAIN ISN'T WORKING RIGHT...
MAYBE IT'S NOT THAT I DIDN'T KNOW.
I MIGHT'VE JUST BEEN PRETENDING NOT TO.
I WISH I HAD MORE TIME...

ANYWAY, THERE'S ONLY...
...ONE ANSWER I COULD EVER GIVE YOU.
...SINCE I'M TOO TIRED NOW...
...I WANNA TAKE A NAP IF THAT'S OKAY.
AFTER MY NAP, IF I FEEL BETTER...
IF I'M NOT TOO SLEEPY, LIKE I AM NOW...
...I'LL GIVE YOU AN ANSWER.
...SO YOU HAVE TO TELL ME THEN...
...I WANT TO TELL YOU...
FINE.
I'LL WAIT FOR YOU TO WAKE UP...
......
YOU DO SEEM REALLY TIRED...

...THAT I LIKE YOU TOO...
...THAT YOU LIKE ME.

빠앙~
BBAAANG
(HONNNK)

HAVE YOU BEEN OUT HERE IN THE COLD ALL ALONG, HEE-SO?
YOU FINALLY MADE IT, HUH, BEATRICE?

IT'S ALREADY DECEMBER.
FINAL EXAMS ARE COMING UP. SHOULDN'T YOU STUDY?
DON'T WORRY. YOU KNOW I HAVE THE BASICS DOWN.
...THAT'S THE PROBLEM. YOU ONLY HAVE THE BASICS AND NOTHING ELSE.
THERE YOU GO AGAIN, YOU STICKLER!
HEE-SO STOPS BY THE HOSPITAL AFTER SCHOOL.

HERE'S TODAY'S MUSIC!!
MP3
KPod
AGAIN?
WHENEVER SHE COMES TO THE HOSPITAL, SHE BRINGS A LOT OF LOUD MUSIC.
DON'T STAY TOO LONG TODAY, AND MAKE SURE YOU GO HOME AND STUDY.
OKAY, OKAY.
DON'T READ YOUR TRASHY ROMANCE NOVELS.
SHUWOO (FWSSSH)
I WON'T, I WON'T. GEEZ.

AND SHE LISTENS TO IT WITH MY MASTER.
THAT'S TOO LOUD. AREN'T YOU HURTING YOUR EARS?
BUT...
...I DON'T KNOW HOW ELSE TO WAKE HIM UP.
HE PROMISED ME.

BUT MY MASTER HASN'T WOKEN UP FOR TWO MONTHS.
HE SAID HE'D ANSWER ME...
...WHEN HE WAKES UP.

13th BOY

IT'S GOTTEN TOO COLD...
FINAL EXAMS ARE OVER.
TOMORROW IS CHRISTMAS EVE.
UGH~! I BOUGHT A COUPLE PRESENTS, AND NOW I ONLY HAVE A FEW COINS LEFT.
CHRISTMAS AND NEW YEAR'S MAKE US ALL SUFFER.
WHAT DID YOU BUY?
UMM...
A BOX OF CHOCO PIE FOR HEE-JEE, A HANDKER-CHIEF FOR MY TEACHER—
A CELL PHONE CHARM FOR NAM-JOO.
AN "EXPENSIVE" HAIRPIN WITH LOTS OF BLING FOR HEE-JOO.
YOU KNOW... YOU ALWAYS SPEND MORE ON HEE-JOO.
I DON'T HAVE A CHOICE IF I WANT MY NEXT YEAR TO BE PEACEFUL.
OTHERWISE I'LL GET A "LOVE BEATING" FROM HER.
ㅠㅅㅠ
WHY?
MY DAD'S IN TROUBLE THIS YEAR.

AS YOU KNOW, EVERY YEAR WE THREE SISTERS DECLARE OUR WISHES FROM THE BACKYARD TO THE SANTA IN THE LIVING ROOM.
ARE YOU ALL READY?!!
YES, MA'AM!
CHUK (TAK)
ROGER !!
SANTA CLAUS! WE THREE SISTERS HAVE ONCE AGAIN GATHERED TOGETHER...
...TO PROCLAIM OUR CHRISTMAS WISHES!!
HEE-JOO EUN WANTS A LAPTOP FOR HER SCHOOL-WORK—!!
HEE-SO EUN WANTS A NINTENDO DS TO TRAIN HER BRAIN~!!
JJURUNG (CLOUD)
JJURUNG
HEE-JEE, WHO GOT FIRST PLACE IN SCHOOL, WANTS A CELL PHONE ~!
THERE THEY GO AGAIN—
MR. EUN WILL HAVE TO WORK HARD AGAIN THIS YEAR.
THANK GOD I ONLY HAVE ONE CHILD.
PLEASE, SANTA CLAUS!!
WE'RE WISHING ~!!
WH-WHAT SHOULD WE DO ...?
YOUNG-MAHN EUN, WHO DIDN'T GET HIS PROMOTION
THEY OUGHTA BE THRASHED UNTIL THEY CAN THINK STRAIGHT!!

HOW COULD YOU ASK FOR SUCH PRICEY THINGS?
YOUR DAD MUST BE HAVING A HARD TIME.
IT'S IMPOSSIBLE TO GET WHAT WE WANT ANYWAY, SO WE PUT FORWARD SOMETHING EXPENSIVE FIRST AND THEN NEGOTIATE.
WELL, IT MIGHT BE DIFFERENT FOR HEE-JEE SINCE SHE TOOK FIRST PLACE IN SCHOOL.
AH! CLOSE YOUR EYES AND LOWER YOUR HEAD, BEATRICE.
WHY—? ARE YOU GOING TO HIT ME...?
WHY WOULD I HIT YOU WHEN YOU HAVEN'T DONE ANYTHING WRONG?
JUST LOWER YOUR HEAD!!
O-OKAY...
꾸벅
KOOBUK (DOWN)
SSK (TUG)
THERE—

I...I DON'T HAVE ANYTHING FOR YOU, THOUGH...
IT'S YOUR EARLY CHRISTMAS PRESENT.
WE MIGHT NOT GET TO SEE EACH OTHER AGAIN UNTIL THE NEW YEAR.
ANYWAY, IT'S THE FIRST TIME I'VE GIVEN YOU A CHRISTMAS GIFT, RIGHT?
NOW THAT YOU'RE HUMAN, THERE'S A LOT OF OPTIONS. I'M GLAD TO SEE IT FITS.
IT'S SNOWING!!
IT'S THE FIRST SNOW OF THE YEAR!!
AH!!
I- I'LL GIVE HEE-SO A PRESENT TOO!!
NO NEED. JUST BE WELL AND STAY PRETTY LIKE YOU ARE NOW~! ♥
B- BUT...

SNOW...
ISN'T IT THE FIRST TIME YOU'VE FELT SNOW, BEATRICE?
YES. THOUGH I'VE SEEN IT OFTEN ENOUGH.
RIGHT. YOU WERE LOCKED INSIDE AND ONLY CAME OUT ONCE A MONTH WITH MY OKAY—
BESIDES THIS, THERE HAVE BEEN A LOT OF FIRSTS FOR ME.
ANY FIRST IS EXCITING AND INTERESTING. IT BECOMES MEMORY TO B TREASURED, SO BE SURE TO MAKE THE MOST OF IT.
I HOPE THE SNOW STICKS SO WE CAN HAVE A SNOWBALL FIGHT!

RUNNING IN THE RAIN...
...THE BURNING SUMMER SUN...
...SEEING DRAGONFLIES BLANKET THE SKY...
...AND FALLEN LEAVES SCATTERING CHAOTICALLY...
...AND THE SNOW RIGHT NOW...
THEY'RE ALL MEANINGFUL...
...BUT NOT BECAUSE THEY WERE FIRSTS FOR ME.
THE REASON THESE MOMENTS ARE PRECIOUS...
...IS BECAUSE I GOT TO BE WITH YOU.
THE FLAKES ARE SETTLING ON YOUR HEAD.
TOODOOK (BRUSH)
YOURS TOO!

AND MAYBE...

...IT'S ALSO BECAUSE THERE MIGHT NOT BE A SECOND TIME...

IT LOOKS LIKE IT'LL SNOW ALL NIGHT.
SSS (FSSH)
HEE-SO.
THE REASON...
...MASTER CAN'T WAKE UP...
...MIGHT BE ME.

MASTER KNEW ABOUT IT.
SO THEN WHY...?
THE POWER CAME WITH A PRICE.
WHY COULDN'T HE STOP...
...UNTIL HE ENDED UP LIKE THIS...?

MASTER...
IS THERE ANYTHING...
...I CAN DO FOR MASTER...?
꽈악
KWAAK (CLUTCH)
PLEASE TELL ME...
...WHAT I SHOULD DO.

WHERE AM I?
I JUST FELL ASLEEP...
매앰맴맴맴...
MAMMAMMAMMAMMAM
두리번
DOORIBUN
두리번
DOORIBUN (PEER)
매앰맴맴. 맴맴...
MAMMAMMAMMAMMAM (BZZZZZZZZZZZ)
...WH...
WHAT...?!
IT'S...
...SUMMER?
턱
TUK (TMP)
BUT I WAS JUST IN THE HOSPITAL...
쨍~
JJANG (BLAZE)
ARGH, TOO BRIGHT!
훌렁
WHOOLRUNG (STRIP)
AND TOO HOT!!

......
EH...?
SSR (SHK)
OWWWW~! WHAT DID I TRIP ON?
으아앗!!
AUGH!!
KOODANG (WHUMP)
IS HE...
YOU'RE FINALLY BACK...
BUT YOU TOOK TOO LONG.

THIS IS THE DEEPEST PART OF HIS CONSCIOUSNESS.
AND I'M THE SOURCE OF THE POWER HE HAS.
M-MASTER SHRANK ?!!
OHH... OF COURSE YOU ARE!
KUDUK (NOD)
끄덕
KUDUK
끄덕!
EXPLAINING IN A CALM AND ORDERLY FASHION
I'VE ALWAYS BEEN THIS SIZE.
...YOU KNOW NOTHING...
I WONDER HOW YOU GOT HERE.
...PLEASE WAKE MASTER UP!!!
HE'S BEEN SLEEPING FOR THE LAST TWO MONTHS!!
...WAIT! IF THAT'S TRUE...

THE PLACE WE ARE...
...IS LIKE A MENTAL LANDSCAPE CREATED BY HIS SUBCON-SCIOUS MIND.
AND I WAS SLEEPING JUST LIKE HIM UNTIL YOU CAME.
I'VE BEEN LOCKED UP IN HERE ALL ALONG!
WHAT?! WHY IS THAT?
YOU SAID YOU'RE THE SOURCE OF HIS POWER. WAS THAT A LIE?!!
THERE'S NOTHING I CAN DO FOR HIM NOW.
I DON'T HAVE THE POWER TO HELP HIM.
JJANG (BLAZE)
THE LANDSCAPE IS SUPPOSED TO CHANGE WITH HIS FEELINGS, WISHES, AND DREAMS...
...BUT TIME AND SPACE STAND STILL HERE AND HAVE ALWAYS REMAINED THE SAME.
SINCE *THAT DAY,* THIS PLACE HAS BEEN SEALED. AND SO HAVE I.
THAT DAY...? WHEN?

......
THE DAY HE BLINDLY SPLIT UP HIS HEART...
...BY POURING HIS WISH INTO A CACTUS...
...AND GIVING IT THE POWER TO HAVE A WILL OF ITS OWN.
THE DAY YOU CAME INTO BEING FROM HIS HEART AND MY POWER.
BECAUSE HE IGNORED MY WARNING AND THE INHERENT DANGER OF HIS SITUATION...
...HE SLEEPS ON ENDLESSLY...
ULTIMATELY, THAT DAY PROVED FATAL...
...TO BOTH HIM AND TO ME.

......
SO...
...WHAT SHOULD I DO...?
IF HE DOESN'T GET BACK FROM YOU WHAT HE LOST ON THAT FATEFUL DAY...
...HE MIGHT NEVER WAKE UP AGAIN.

BUT IN DOING SO...
...YOU WOULDN'T BE ABLE TO REMAIN IN THAT FORM.
BUT YOU DO.
YOU COULD RETURN HIS HEART TO ME VOLUNTARILY.
I DON'T HAVE ANY POWER LEFT...
...TO DO ANYTHING FOR HIM MYSELF.
IT'S UP TO YOU.
I WON'T FORCE OR BEG YOU.
EVERYTHING WOULD GO BACK TO HOW IT WAS.
...BACK TO HOW IT WAS...
YOU DON'T NEED TO GIVE UP ALL YOU HAVE NOW...
...IF YOU JUST IGNORE THE BOY WHO NEVER OPENS HIS EYES.

SARAK (FALLS)
사락
THE CHOICE IS YOURS.
SARAK
사락
WE DON'T HAVE MUCH TIME.
IF I FALL ASLEEP AND AM UNABLE TO WAKE UP TOO...
...THEN NO ONE WILL BE ABLE TO WAKE HIM.
IF YOU DON'T PAY HIM ANY MIND, YOU CAN HAVE A LIFE AS YOU ARE NOW.

THE SNOW STUCK OVERNIGHT.
TODAY'S CHRISTMAS EVE, THE DAY BEFORE A WHITE CHRISTMAS.
WHAT'S UP WITH COMING HERE SO EARLY?
IT'S 10 A.M.
I SAID I COULDN'T HANG OUT WITH YOU TODAY.
후아앙..
HUAHHHH (YAWN)
I KNOW, I KNOW.
I JUST CAME TO SEE YOU FOR A SECOND.
I'LL HAVE TIME FOR YOU THE DAY AFTER.
I'M HAVING A PARTY WITH FRIENDS LATER.
AND THERE'S A FAMILY GATHERING WITH MY AUNTS TOMORROW.

찰칵
CHALKACK (SNAP)
EH...?
찰칵
CHALKACK
WHAT'S THAT? A DIGITAL CAMERA?
I FOUND IT WHILE I WAS CLEANING MASTER'S ROOM. I ALWAYS WANTED TO TAKE SOME PICTURES.
SO I BROUGHT IT OVER.
찰칵
CHALKACK
찰칵
CHALKACK
찰칵
CHALKACK
OKAY, THAT'S ENOUGH—
찰칵
CHALKACK
IT'S HARD TO DO SEXY POSES-!
HEY, YOU SURE IT'S OKAY TO TAKE HIS STUFF WITHOUT PERMISSION?
SO? MASTER'S SLEEPING ANYWAY.
찰칵
CHALKACK
WHATEVER I DO, HE WON'T KNOW ABOUT IT.

......
찰칵
CHALKACK
CAN'T I ACT FOR MY OWN PLEASURE?
CAN'T I DO WHAT I WANT?
HUH? WHAT? THAT'S NOT LIKE YOU, SO WHAT'S UP?
RESPONDS TO THE CAMERA INSTINCTIVELY
찰칵
CHALKACK (SNAP)
THEN CAN I TAKE AS MANY PICTURES AS I WANT?
찰칵
CHALKACK
YOU'RE MOODY 'COS I WON'T PLAY WITH YOU, HUH? OKAY, OKAY. YOU CAN DO WHATEVER YOU WANT UNTIL THE PARTY.
찰칵
CHALKACK
찰칵
CHALKACK
HEY!!
DON'T DO THAT!!
찰칵
CHALKACK
치카
CHIKA (BRUSH)
치카
CHIKA
쏴아
SHWAAAH (SPLASH)

YOU'RE UNBELIEVABLE.
WHEN ARE YOU GONNA BE SATISFIED? YOU'D BETTER DELETE THE PHOTOS LATER!
찰칵
CHALKACK
JOOWOOK (SQUEEZE)
LOTION
THE PARTY STARTS AT TWO, OKAY? I HAVE TO HEAD OUT THIRTY MINUTES EARLY.
OKAY.
WELL, SINCE YOU'RE HERE...
...HELP ME WITH MY CLOTHES AND HAIR!
THIS OR THIS...
WHICH ONE'S BETTER?
UMM~! I LIKE THE ONE ON THE RIGHT, THE BEIGE.
THIS ONE? 'KAY~! ♥
...HEE-SO.
CAN I ASK YOU ONE THING?

WHERE'D I PUT MY STOCKINGS?
WHAT IS IT?
IF ONLY ONE OF US COULD STAY WITH YOU AND THE OTHER HAD TO DISAPPEAR...
...WOULD YOU CHOOSE MASTER OR ME?
WHAT?
WHY'RE YOU ASKING ME SUCH A RIDICULOUS QUESTION?
ARE YOU COMPARING YOURSELF TO WHIE-YOUNG?
I KNOW, HUH? IT'S SO STUPID OF ME, RIGHT?
THE ANSWER IS CLEAR.
YEAH, IT'S CLEAR!!
찰칵
CHALKACK (SNAP)
STOP SHOOTING!!
I'M ONLY WEARING UNDER-WEAR...!!

......
WHY? WHY ME?
I'M... ASHAMED THAT YOU'D EVEN HAVE TO ASK ME SOMETHING SO OBVIOUS...
WHO ELSE WOULD IT BE BUT YOU?
FIRST OF ALL, I CAN'T PUT YOU IN THE SAME CAT-EGORY...
...AS WHIE-YOUNG.
IT'S DIFFERENT.
BUT YOU LIKE MASTER.
OH MY...;;
...WHY...?
SO WHY WOULD YOU CHOOSE ME?

SO IT'S POINTLESS TO COMPARE YOU TO ANYONE OR ANYTHING ELSE.
BECAUSE YOUR EXISTENCE IS NON-NEGOTIABLE.
RIGHT... TO HEE-SO...
...A
RIGHT.
DIDN'T YOU KNOW THAT, YOU IDIOT?

...I'M A PRECIOUS PART OF HER WORLD...
...THAT SHOULD NEVER LEAVE HER.
BUT IF IT'S POINTLESS TO COMPARE ME TO ANYONE...
...THEN THAT MEANS I CAN NEVER BE IN THE SAME CATEGORY...
...AS A MAN SHE LIKES.
DARN, I FORGOT TO WASH THEM.
I GOTTA BORROW HEE-JOO'S.
KOORI (DIRTY)
꾸리
KOORI
꾸리
I CAN NEVER BE A MAN TO HEE-SO.
(ESPECIALLY CONSIDERING SHE'S FINE WITH HAVING NOTHING BUT UNDERWEAR ON IN FRONT OF ME...;;;)

SO...

...THE MAN WHO MAKES HEE-SO HAPPY...

...ISN'T ME.

YOU'VE PUT UP A HUGE STOCKING.

IS THAT FOR YOUR DAD'S GIFT...?

IT'S STRETCHY TOO.

HE SEEMS TO BE PLANNING ON DRESSING UP AS SANTA AGAIN THIS YEAR.

I ALWAYS FALL ASLEEP THE MINUTE MY HEAD HITS THE PILLOW...

...SO I'M NOT SURE IF I CAN STAY AWAKE UNTIL HE COMES WITH MY PRESENT.

GOOD FOR YOU, HEE-SO ~!

YOUNG-MAHN EUN HAS PUT ON WEIGHT SINCE LAST YEAR

IT'S A LITTLE TIGHT...

YOU'RE GETTIN FAT! DO SOME-THING ABOUT THAT GU WOULD YOU?!!

I TOLD YOU THERE'S NO NEED.
DON'T WASTE YOUR MONEY ON ME.
IT'S TOO SMALL?!
...I...
...WANT TO GIVE YOU A CHRISTMAS GIFT TOO.
A CHRISTMAS GIFT...
IT WON'T...? THEN WHAT IS IT?
IT'S NOT AN I.O.U. COUPON FOR A MASSAGE OR SOME-THING, IS IT?
I FINALLY GOT IT ZIPPED.
IT WON'T COST ANY MONEY.

HEE-SO EUN'S DESTINY.

......
WHAT THE HECK DOES THAT MEAN?
HE'S BEEN TALKING CRAZY ALL DAY...
SANGUL (SMILE)
THAT'S MY CHRISTMAS GIFT TO YOU.
BUT I...
...WILL MAKE IT SO YOU MEET FOR SURE.
ARE YOU TEASING ME?
NO, I'M BEING VERY SERIOUS.
YOU ARE, HUH... SO ARE YOU GONNA SET ME UP ON A BLIND DATE OR SOMETHING?
WELL... WHO CAN SAY...?

THAT'S THE ONLY PRESENT I CAN GIVE TO YOU...

THE END OF VOLUME 11
TO BE CONTINUED AND COMPLETED IN 13TH BOY, VOLUME 12!

13th Boy

WANNA KNOW WHAT KINDA STORY'S THE BONUS IN THIS VOLUME~? TAKE A LOOK AT THE NEXT PAGE!

THE STORY OF THE GREASY-HAIRED CREATOR OF <13TH BOY>!! LET'S TAKE A QUICK LOOK!!
WHY SHOULD WE?
FOR A FEW YEARS NOW, CREATOR LEE HAS BEEN GOING TO INSTITUTIONS OF LEARNING FOR HER OWN ENJOYMENT, RATHER THAN FOR SELF-DEVELOPMENT OR KNOWLEDGE-BUILDING.
I SHOULDN'T JUST STAY HOME! LET'S GO AND LEARN SOMETHING!!
IT'D BE A PROBLEM IF I GOT ANY SMARTER, THOUGH... ;;
THE FIRST THING SHE STARTED WITH WAS "JAPANESE"!
SOOLSOOLSOOL (FLUENT)
O-GENKI DESU KA~ YAMETE~
HER GOAL WAS TO READ A JAPANESE COMIC BOOK!
KONNICHIWA~ ARIGATOU~ AISHITERU~
OISHII JAPANESE
A YEAR AND HALF LATER...
Victory!!
WOW~! YES, I'M A GENIUS!!
PEOPLE USUALLY GET IT IN SIX MONTHS.
...SHE PASSED THE JLPT, LEVEL 3!!

BUT SHE WAS BORN WITH A TENDENCY TO IZZLE OUT, SO HER INTEREST TRAILED OFF QUICKLY!!
THERE'S NOTHING MORE TO LEARN ABOUT JAPANESE. LET'S LOOK INTO SOME-THING ELSE.
YOU'VE JUST LEARNED GREETINGS, AND THERE'S NOTHING MORE TO LEARN?!
HEH!
YOU'RE TOTALLY CKING IN NACITY!!
AND SHE FOUND A DRAMA WRITING SCHOOL WHILE SURFING ONLINE!!
OH! THERE'S A CLASS FOR THIS KINDA STUFF?
BUNDDUK (FLASH)
번뜩
CREATOR LEE WATCHES DRAMAS, SO...
...THERE SHE WENT WITH HER FANTASTIC DELUSIONS AGAIN!!
YES! I'M A COMIC BOOK WRITER! WHY CAN'T I WRITE DRAMA?!
I GOTTA GO FOR ONE SOURCE, MULTI-USE!!
DO YOU EVEN KNOW THE MEANING OF THIS?;;
IF YOU DO, IT'LL BE GARBAGE!!
SHE APPLIED, TOOK THE NTERVIEW, AND PASSED!
TOUGH ADMISSION PROCESS...;;
FINALLY SHE BECAME A WOULD-BE DRAMA WRITER!
WELL-BEGUN IS HALF-DONE, WHICH MEANS I'M ALMOST DONE~!
LET'S MEET THROUGH A DRAMA NEXT TIME, READERS!!
SHE'S EASILY SWAYED.
DRAMA!
BUT SHE MISSED CLASSES WHENEVER SHE HAD A DEADLINE, AND SHE'D FALL ASLEEP IN CLASS AND NEVER DO THE WORK...
AWW... I'VE MISSED HALF THE CLASSES. MY MONEY ~!
SHE'S FINISHING UP <13TH BOY>...
BECAUSE OF ALL HER ABSENCES, SHE COULDN'T MOVE UP TO THE NEXT LEVEL!
YOU'VE BLOWN THAT MONEY.
HOW WASTEFUL...
DAMN...
ON TOP OF THAT, SHE'D TAKEN CLASSES IN THE PAINTER PROGRAM, ILLUSTRATION, SWIMMING, ETC., BUT SHE COULDN'T FINISH ANY OF THEM...
DUHUK (GASP)
더헉
AH...I MIGHT GO BANKRUPT FROM ALL THE TUITION FEES~!
BANK BOOK
SO THE CONCLUSION WAS!!
I'LL ONLY DO COMIC BOOKS!! I'LL FINISH THEM A WEEK BEFORE THE DEADLINE!!
AND THAT'S THE LIFE STORY OF CREATOR LEE...♪
NO ONE WILL BELIEVE YOU!!

★ SPECIAL THANKS!
- MY MOM
- WORLD-CLASS PRO ASSISTANT BABYBOX
- KIMBAB HEAVEN AND HANDMADE BLACK NOODLES FROM HONG-KYU JANG

THIS BOOK IS DEDICATED TO BABYBOX, WHO SUPPORTED MY WEAK DRAWING WITH HER SPECTACULAR TONING TECHNIQUE. (=人=;; MIMICKING OTHER FAMOUS BOOKS)

PS: I DREW SOMETHING SEXY FOR YOU SINCE YOU GO WILD FOR SUGGESTIVE NUDITY. WHAT AN EMBARRASSING MOMENT. ㅠ人ㅠ WHATEVER YOU DO AND WHEREVER YOU GO, I WISH YOU THE BEST OF LUCK. YOU GO, GIRL!!

13th Boy

Page 63
Kimchi: A traditional fermented Korean dish made of vegetables with varied seasonings.

Page 174
***Konnichiwa*:** Japanese for "Hello."
***Arigatou*:** Japanese for "Thank you."
***Aishiteru*:** Japanese for "I love you."

***Ogenki desu ka*:** Japanese for "Are you well?"
***Yamete*:** Japanese for "Stoppp!"

***Oishii* Japanese:** The book title translates to *Tasty Japanese*.

JLPT: Japanese Language Proficiency Test

LET'S MEET ONE LAST TIME IN VOLUME 12, THE FINAL VOLUME OF 13TH BOY~!

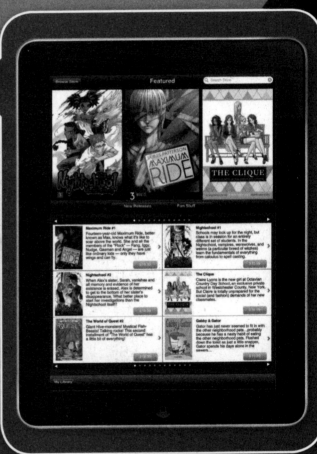

13th BOY ⑪

SANGEUN LEE

Translation: JiEun Park
English Adaptation: Natalie Baan

Lettering: Terri Delgado

This book is a work of fiction. Names, characters, places, and incidents are the product of the author's imagination or are used fictitiously. Any resemblance to actual events, locales, or persons, living or dead, is coincidental.

The characters and events in this book are fictitious. Any similarity to real persons, living or dead, is coincidental and not intended by the author.

Yen Press
Hachette Book Group
237 Park Avenue, New York, NY 10017

www.HachetteBookGroup.com
www.YenPress.com

Yen Press is an imprint of Hachette Book Group, Inc.
The Yen Press name and logo are trademarks of Hachette Book Group, Inc.

First Yen Press Edition: March 2012

ISBN: 978-0-316-19082-4

10 9 8 7 6 5 4 3 2 1

BVG

Printed in the United States of America